# The RV Log Book and Journal

Waterlane
e d i t i o n s

Vancouver/Toronto

Reviewed by Peter Clark and Warren Clark
Edited by Elaine Jones
Proofread by Lisa Collins
Book design by Roberta Batchelor
Front cover map supplied by ©Informap
from the Ontario Road and Recreation Atlas

Printed and bound in Canada.

**Canadian Cataloguing in Publication Data**

Elmer, Howard
The RV Log Book and Journal

   ISBN 1-55285-016-1

   1. Recreational vehicles. 2. Recreational vehicle living. 3. Diaries
(Blank-books) I. Title.
TX110.E45 2000        796.7'9        C00-910636-7


The publisher acknowledges the support of the Canada Council for the
Arts and the Cultural Services Branch of the Government of British Columbia for our
publishing program. We acknowledge the financial support of the Government of
Canada through the Book Industry Development Program for our publishing activities.

# Contents

# Introduction

An RVer is part of a fraternity that bridges cultural and economic boundaries with a common love of adventure and freedom. Elusive themes, and ones that often present themselves at surprising moments. It might happen on a sun-drenched summer day in the mountains or a cold starry night in the desert, or perhaps as you're tucking in your family on a stormy, dirty night. Wherever the spirit touches you, it will be unique and exclusive, but it will also have three familiar threads: first, you'll realize that in RVing, like life, the journey is the thing; second, you do have to leave home to find it; and third, you are not alone.

RV folks come from every walk of life and corner of the globe. They are part of a truly unique North American phenomenon—people traveling down the road only for the sake of traveling, a concept that not that long ago might have been considered strange and wasteful. Though RVs can be found in most every country in the world today, the concept was born here. First it was a necessity, then it was a convenience and now it has become a lifestyle choice.

The history of this century is one of migration. Waves of immigrants came, fanned out across the continent and settled the land. That historical trend fits hand-in-glove with the RV lifestyle.

Starting as early as the turn of the century, RVs had a completely practical application. The amenities that were carried were necessities, primarily because roadside services for travelers simply didn't exist. The automobile and the newly built road network took care of that in succeeding decades, but there was still little or nothing in the way of food, fuel or accommodation available outside of towns. As the need to carry your own bed and supplies waned, the joys of getting off the beaten path started to gain in popularity.

Today there are more services available than any of us will ever need, yet the popularity of RVing has never been greater. So, why don't people just stay in motels and eat at any of the multitude of fast-food restaurants clogging highway interchanges, instead of struggling with unwieldy, titanic-sized vehicles?

If you own an RV you know the answer; if you're reading this book and thinking about an RV you already suspect. The RV inspires in us the pioneer, the independent adventurer. It gives us, in a word, freedom—the same ideal that brought many of our forebears to these shores.

## On Board Systems Check

### AUXILIARY BATTERY
- check connections for corrosion
- observe fluid level in cells
- if checking with a hydrometer, for most batteries 1.270 is a full charge reading

### INTERIOR LIGHTS
- try them all, on DC (house battery), connected to shore power (AC), and with the generator running (if so equipped)

## LP Gas System

All liquid propane systems are made up of three parts: the supply, the delivery system and the appliances. Checking the system is composed of answering these three questions.
- is there propane in the tank?
- does the propane flow to the appliances?
- do the appliances light and work?

If you're concerned about a leak, follow your nose. Propane has an unmistakable odor. If you suspect a leak, brush a soap and water solution on the valve, fitting or line. It will reveal the leak by producing bubbles where the gas is escaping. Don't attempt to repair gas systems yourself. Take them to a qualified RV mechanic.

**TIP**

By checking systems in the same order each time you will create a habit—one more assurance that a crucial check won't be missed.

## The Water System

At the end of your last trip you should have dumped all the tanks (including the fresh water), so you will be starting out empty. Remember that stagnant water can grow algae. You can dump this water, but plastic water tanks can absorb the odor and contaminate the next fill-up.

Start by filling your fresh water tank from a known source. Once full, run the pump and open all the taps to run water into the lines and the hot water tank. This will also purge the air from the lines. Dump some water into the toilet, shower and sink traps to prevent odors from rising up through the plumbing.

Make a habit of doing the following.
- keep your fresh water full
- visually check the water lines and demand pump for leaks
- make sure fill valves are closed when not in use

**TIP**

A teaspoon of bleach put into the fill hose just before you turn on the city water will sanitize the hose and tank as you flush the system. A water purifier attached to the kitchen tap is also a good investment.

## The Waste Tanks

Dump your waste as often as possible. It's that simple.

If possible, always dump your tanks before traveling any distance, because with the sloshing around you are bound to get some odors coming back into the RV. All the more reason to use deodorant at the start of the trip, even if the tanks are empty. This will condition the tanks and keep things under control when they begin to fill. Keep the dump station and dump hose clean. It takes a few extra minutes but you will be paid back in spades when you don't have to struggle with a dirty, smelly hose. Most folks want to get away from the dump station as quickly as possible, and this is understandable, but pay special attention to how your dump valves are working. Dump valves can jam and get stuck; if they feel sticky spend a few extra minutes and run water into them while working them back and forth.

Before you set out, check the following.

- dump valves closed and dump caps on and sealed
- dump hose clean and in place
- tanks empty
- deodorant added
- water run into all plumbing traps and the toilet bowl

**TIP**

When you are hooked up to a campground sewer system, don't leave your dump valves open. Instead, leave your dump hose connected while your tanks fill, but only dump them when they are full. The force of the water will carry the solids and suspended material out of the tank, whereas, if you leave the valves open the water will drain away and leave the solids behind to build up, dry out and clog your tanks.

# Packing

There is a temptation to take everything, including the kitchen sink, along on your RV vacation. And though the cavernous space of your RV may beckon to be filled, just remember it all adds to the total weight that you have to carry or tow. So fight the urge to overpack. (Besides, you already have a kitchen sink.)

All RVs have a GVWR (gross vehicle weight rating). This is the total weight of the unit, gear and people, as recommended by the manufacturer. They will also give you a "dry" weight, or the weight of the unloaded unit on its own. The difference between the two is what you are allowed to pack in. At some point it is a good idea to weigh the RV on a truck scale, loaded (including water and propane), to find out how much weight you're carrying.

Weight is one thing, but the other (and most often overlooked) fact is that all that gear is going to be moving. And, I assure you, gravity works exceptionally well in RVs. So, here are the rules.

- put light stuff on top
- stow heavy items down below
- secure all cupboard doors
- latch the fridge door and any other such equipped doors
- don't leave loose items on the counter or table

**TIP**

**When opening any door (in transit or otherwise) do so s-l-o-w-l-y and prepare for something to fall out, particularly from the fridge.**

# The Campground Checkout

Getting set up in a campsite is probably the easiest and quickest of any RV chore. You'll need the services and you'll want to get hooked up quickly so you can get on to having fun or just kicking back. Detailing the setup here is unnecessary.

Not so with checkout the next morning. With a brand new RV day dawning, everyone is anxious to hit the road, and this is when the majority of disasters strike. Many an RVer has had his electrical and sewer hose amputated in his hurry to leave, or left his TV antenna hanging from a tree branch. No, the quick getaway is often costly. Make your checkout routine the same as your setup and pretrip—thorough and the same every time.

These are the basics of the checkout.
- LP gas off (unless otherwise equipped)
- water pump switch off
- water in drains and toilet
- all doors closed and latched (including outside "basement storage" doors)
- roof vents closed
- windows closed
- TV antenna down
- electrical, sanitary and fresh water hoses disconnected and stowed
- engine check, brake check, walk around lights check
- steps retracted, hitches checked
- landing gear or stabilizers up and locked
- slideout rooms retracted and locked

**TIP**

To get the job done quickly, make each family member responsible for an aspect of the checkout routine. Just before takeoff, have each person sound off and confirm that their job is done.

# Safety

The catch phrase "safety first" should apply to every RV adventure. The RV, by its very nature, can carry you far from the nearest medical facility or repair station. And while this is where you want to go, if something goes wrong you must be prepared.

Boondocking, particularly with kids, means there will be cuts and scrapes, sunburns and poison ivy rashes. But with a properly stocked first-aid kit and a little know-how, most minor medical emergencies can be handled in the field.

Taking a Red Cross or St. John Ambulance course is a good investment in peace of mind, and you should have a good first-aid book on hand. Here are some of the items you may want to carry in your own RV first-aid kit.

- adhesive bandages of various sizes
- disinfectant cream
- ice packs
- roller bandage
- large-size sterile pads
- rubbing alcohol
- cotton swabs
- scissors
- tweezers
- safety pins
- pain reliever
- bandage tape
- thermometer

In addition, think along the lines of what you have in your medicine cabinet at home. Things like sunscreen, aloe lotion and moisturizer will be more useful to you in the RV than sitting at home.

Prescription medications are something most people don't forget, but you might forget to take refill instructions and requests for on-the-road use. Medical information that may be vital in a life-threatening situation should also be carried on board. This can include X-rays, Ct scan results and the like.

RVers with allergies must have puffers, bee sting kits or other anaphylactic shock antidotes on hand. At least one other person should know how to administer them in case the patient is unable to.

**TIP**

Slowly duplicate these items so you can leave them in the RV. This way you won't forget anything and you'll save yourself the bother of packing and unpacking each time you travel.

Lastly, have all your medical information and contact phone numbers written down on one sheet of paper. Make copies, which can be given to any attending medical personnel to make their job easier and more efficient. Be prepared, have fun, be safe.

# The Mechanical Emergency

Most RVs today are efficient and for the most part trouble free. But there will always be the need for minor adjustments and repairs, so a well-stocked tool kit should be a priority. That tool kit could save you a big tow bill by keeping you going till you can get to a service center. The items that follow are must-haves for your tool kit.

- socket wrench set, 3/8- or 1/2-inch drive
- screwdrivers
- pliers: needlenose, adjustable, electrical
- claw hammer
- crowbar
- duct tape
- open-end wrench set
- adjustable wrench
- crimping and wire-stripping tool
- flashlight
- hacksaw
- tire pressure gauge
- circuit tester
- electrical tape
- utility knife
- lubricant, such as WD-40

**TIP**

If you don't have a particular tool, chances are one of your neighbors in the campground does. Just be prepared for a lot of free advice with the loan of the tool.

Other items you will want to have on hand are:

- extra fuses
- road flares
- jumper cables
- a spare gas can
- extra motor oil
- jack
- fire extinguisher

# Choosing a Campground

Before you start looking for a campground, be specific about your personal needs.
- how long will you be staying?
- what services and facilities do you require?
- if the campground is to be used as a base of operations, how will you get around?
- do you require special facilities?
- are reservations required?

Begin your search with your needs in mind. You can always settle for less, but why should you if you don't have to?

Campground guides will be your primary source of information for choosing a campsite. These are varied and are available from many different sources. The obvious ones, such as government park listings, can be found at dozens of locations. There are also private campground associations that publish their own listings. Also look for listings supplied by travel and camping magazines and large chains, such as Kampgrounds of America (KOA). And don't forget the internet; here you can not only get campground information but can often see what the place looks like before you ever set foot in it. Then, if you like it, you can make reservations right on-line.

Find out where the amenities are located so you can plan where you want to be. For example, with small children you'll want to be right by the playground, so you can watch them from your site and so they don't have far to go. If you don't have kids, the opposite will hold true. You'll want to park far from the playground because it's a noisy place. See how that works? The same holds for the comfort station, pool, laundry, adjacent roads, etc. From a technical viewpoint, you need to know about power, water, sewer, phone and cable or dish availability. Think about whether you'll need full hookups for a longer stay, or whether dry camping is more appropriate if you will have your unit in and out of the park often. You'll also want to know the maximum length of RV allowed, whether they have pull-through sites (no backing up), length of stay allowed and access to surrounding attractions. In a word, know your needs.

Campground guides go hand in hand with a good road atlas. Government road maps are fine, but investing in a comprehensive road atlas will pay dividends. These have a wealth of information over and above basic highway description, such as tourism addresses and phone numbers and points of interest. Some even offer what's known as truckers' routing tips. These identify stretches of road that are not suitable for large or articulated vehicles—handy information indeed.

## Some Club and Campground Resources

### National Association of RV Parks and Campgrounds
8605 Westwood Center Drive, Suite 201
Vienna, VA  22182-2231
Tel: 703-734-3000
Fax: 703-734-3004

This association of more than 3,000 RV parks and campgrounds is dedicated to providing training and support to ensure its members run professional, safe, friendly sites.

### The Family Motor Coach Association (FMCA)
8291 Clough Pike
Cincinnati, OH 45244
513-474-3622
800-543-3622

This is a non-profit association of motor coach owners that offers a monthly magazine, trip routing, road service, message forwarding, conventions and insurance deals to its members.

**Escapees**
100 Rainbow Drive
Livingston, TX  77351
409-327-8873

This club has chapters in the U.S., Canada and Mexico.
It offers the usual services.

**The Good Sam Club**
PO Box 500
Agoura, CA 91376
818-991-4980
800-234-3450

This is the largest camping/RV club in the world. It offers a wide variety
of services, many of them available on a worldwide basis.

**National Campers and Hikers Association**
4804 Transit Road, Building 2
Depew, NY  14043-4906
716-668-6242

There are chapters in Canada and the U.S. offering discounts, rallies,
insurance and other services.

# Directories and Guides

## Camping Canada's Campground Directory
2585 Skymark Ave. Unit 306
Mississauga, ON  L4W 4L5
905-624-8218
Published as one issue of the magazine it covers over
4,000 campgrounds coast to coast in Canada.

## KOA Directory/Road Atlas/Camping Guide
Kampgrounds of America
PO Box 30162, Billings, MT 59107-0162
406-248-7444
Lists KOA locations worldwide.

## Trailer Life Campground & RV Services Directory
TL Enterprises
29901 Agoura Road, Agoura, CA 91301
818-991-4980
Listings in Canada, Mexico and the U.S., along with maps and
other information.

## Woodall's Campground Directories
Woodall's Publishing Co.
PO Box 5000, Lake Forest, IL 60045-5000
800-323-9076
Listings include all of North America and eastern or western editions
can be purchased. In addition to campgrounds, there are maps and other
useful on-the-road information.

# Travel Log

Date *April 21, 2005 (Thurs)*     Mileage start

Weather today                     Mileage ~~end~~  *9.0 mpg*

Fueled at *Flying J*   Price *2.07 / 135.00*   Odometer reading *52,980*
*Wytheville, VA*                   *Propane  1.89 / 35.00*

We stayed at   *Pomykacz's*        Cost

This was a great place because


*We did not pull a car on this trip.*

It could use some help in these areas

~~We were asso~~




We met                            From where

Address and phone number

Groceries                                   Cost

Restaurant  *Flying J*                       Cost

Activities  *Driving*                        Cost

*Lap top computer games*

The best deal of the day                     Cost


The worst deal of the day                    Cost



Today's Adventures  *We drove straight through to*
*Joe + Diane's in Charlotte, N.C.*

Date _April 22, 2005 (Fri)_    Mileage start

Weather today    Mileage end **10**.9 mpg

Fueled at _Flying J_    Price _2.10 / 92.75_    Odometer reading
_Brunswick, GA_

We stayed at _Fort Wilderness / WDW_    Cost $72.00

~~This was a great place because~~ _It was all Night Grad
Night at Magic Kingdom. The buses just
poured in like crazy._

It could use some help in these areas

_We were assigned sites in the 800 loop
that were too small to get into. We were
reassigned to sites 524 and Pomys 523._

We met    From where

Address and phone number

Groceries                                Cost

Restaurant *Flying J / Longhorn*       Cost

Activities     *Driving*                    Cost

The best deal of the day              Cost

The worst deal of the day             Cost

Today's Adventures *Drove to Disney World's Fort Wilderness. We ended up in the 500 loop (which is the premium pet section) at no extra charge because the 800 loop did not work for us. Site number 524 is very, very nice. Site 522 seemed very nice also.*

# TRAVEL LOG

Date *April 23, 2005 (Sat)*     Mileage start

Weather today                   Mileage end

Fueled at          Price         Odometer reading

We stayed at *Fort Wilderness*    Cost  72.36

This was a great place because

_____

_____

It could use some help in these areas

_____

_____

_____

We met                          From where

Address and phone number

_____

_____

_____

| Groceries | | Cost |
|---|---|---|
| Restaurant | Flying Flamingo or | Cost |
| Activities | Pink Flamingo | Cost |

| The best deal of the day | Cost |
|---|---|

| The worst deal of the day | Cost |
|---|---|

Today's Adventures We drove to Cape Coral to see
Joan, Kristi, Nick, Kayphel and Cole for
the day. We saw Kristi and Nick's house,
we saw were they are going to build their
new house and we saw the condo Joan
is buying. We watched Kayphel play
soccer. We went to Sannibel Island and
had lunch.

Date *April 24, 2005  (Sun)*                    Mileage start

Weather today                                    Mileage end

Fueled at                    Price               Odometer reading


We stayed at *Fort Wilderness*                   Cost

This was a great place because




It could use some help in these areas




We met                                           From where

Address and phone number

Groceries                                    Cost

Restaurant                                   Cost

Activities                                   Cost


The best deal of the day                     Cost


The worst deal of the day                    Cost


Today's Adventures

Date  *April 25, 2005 (mon)*

Mileage start

Weather today

Mileage end

Fueled at                    Price

Odometer reading

We stayed at

Cost

This was a great place because

It could use some help in these areas

We met

From where

Address and phone number

| | Cost |
|---|---|
| Groceries | |
| Restaurant | Cost |
| Activities | Cost |

| | Cost |
|---|---|
| The best deal of the day | |

| | Cost |
|---|---|
| The worst deal of the day | |

Today's Adventures  *Magic Kingdom*
We took the boat from the campground.

## TRAVEL LOG

Date  *April 26, 2005 (Tues)*          Mileage start

Weather today                          Mileage end

Fueled at            Price             Odometer reading


We stayed at                           Cost

This was a great place because



It could use some help in these areas



We met                                 From where

Address and phone number

Groceries

Restaurant  Lunch in Mexico    —    Cost Wonderful

Dinner in UK    —    Cost Wonderful

Activities    Cost

The best deal of the day    Cost

The worst deal of the day    Cost

Today's Adventures  Epcot

Mexico  -  Trio combo

UK    -  Fish & Chips and Bangers & Mash

Date *April 27, 2005 (Wed)*     Mileage start

Weather today     Mileage end

Fueled at     Price     Odometer reading

We stayed at     Cost

This was a great place because

It could use some help in these areas

We met     From where

Address and phone number

| | | |
|---|---|---|
| Groceries | | Cost |
| Restaurant | *Perkins (late lunch)* | Cost |
| Activities | | Cost |

| | |
|---|---|
| The best deal of the day | Cost |

| | |
|---|---|
| The worst deal of the day | Cost |

Today's Adventures *Leisurely day - went to camping World. Perkin's for a late lunch. Old Town. Friendly's to have ice cream instead of dinner. Stopped at Publix on the way home.*

Date    *April 28, 2005 (Thurs.)*    Mileage start

Weather today                        Mileage end

Fueled at              Price         Odometer reading

We stayed at *Fort Wilderness Campground* Cost

This was a great place because

It could use some help in these areas

We met                          From where

Address and phone number

Groceries                                    Cost

Restaurant  *Lunch in Italy*          —        *Good*
            *Dinner in Germany (all you* — Cost *Wonderful*
            *can eat)*

Activities                                   Cost


The best deal of the day                     Cost


The worst deal of the day                    Cost


Today's Adventures  *Epcot*
    *Italy - shared a Pasta trio and Chicken Parm*
    *Germany - All You Can Eat Buffet*

Date **April 29, 2005 (Fri.)**   Mileage start

Weather today **Very nice**   Mileage end

Fueled at   Price   Odometer reading

We stayed at **Fort Wilderness C'ground** Cost

This was a great place because

We found out that Friday is a hopping day at the campground with everyone arriving for the week-end.

It could use some help in these areas

We tried to rent a golf cart, but they were all taken. It was All night Grad night again tonight

We met   From where

Address and phone number

Groceries                                        Cost

Restaurant  *Wilderness Lodge (lunch)* Cost

Activities                                       Cost


The best deal of the day  *We were invited* Cost
*to sit in the front car on the monorail and recieved*
                                        *co-pilot licenses*
The worst deal of the day                 Cost


Today's Adventures *We relaxed the first part of the day
then we went to Wilderness Lodge for lunch.
We drove to the Contemorary Hotel and took the
monorail from there to the Polynesian (sp) to the
Floridian to Magic Kingdom and back. Then
we went to Epcot and back. After that we
went to the Trading Post to get some burgers
and hot dogs to grill for dinner. We left
today open to see mom, but she ended up having
to take care of selling her motorhome.*

39

# TRAVEL LOG

Date _____     Mileage start _____

Weather today _____     Mileage end _____

Fueled at _____ Price _____     Odometer reading _____

We stayed at _____     Cost _____

This was a great place because _____

_____

_____

It could use some help in these areas _____

_____

_____

_____

We met _____     From where _____

Address and phone number _____

_____

_____

_____

Groceries                              Cost

Restaurant                             Cost

Activities                             Cost


The best deal of the day               Cost


The worst deal of the day              Cost


Today's Adventures

## TRAVEL LOG

Date _____          Mileage start _____

Weather today _____          Mileage end _____

Fueled at _____ Price _____          Odometer reading _____


We stayed at _____          Cost _____

This was a great place because _____

_____

_____

It could use some help in these areas _____

_____

_____

_____

We met _____          From where _____

Address and phone number _____

_____

_____

_____

Groceries                                    Cost

Restaurant                                    Cost

Activities                                    Cost


The best deal of the day                      Cost


The worst deal of the day                     Cost


Today's Adventures

## TRAVEL LOG

Date _____    Mileage start _____

Weather today _____    Mileage end _____

Fueled at _____ Price _____    Odometer reading _____

We stayed at _____    Cost _____

This was a great place because _____

_____

_____

It could use some help in these areas _____

_____

_____

We met _____    From where _____

Address and phone number _____

_____

_____

_____

Groceries                                      Cost

Restaurant                                     Cost

Activities                                     Cost


The best deal of the day                       Cost


The worst deal of the day                      Cost


Today's Adventures

## TRAVEL LOG

Date                                           Mileage start

Weather today                                  Mileage end

Fueled at                    Price            Odometer reading


We stayed at                                   Cost

This was a great place because




It could use some help in these areas




We met                                         From where

Address and phone number

Groceries                                    Cost

Restaurant                                   Cost

Activities                                   Cost


The best deal of the day                     Cost


The worst deal of the day                    Cost


Today's Adventures

## TRAVEL LOG

Date                                    Mileage start

Weather today                           Mileage end

Fueled at               Price           Odometer reading


We stayed at                            Cost

This was a great place because



It could use some help in these areas




We met                                  From where

Address and phone number

Groceries                                    Cost

Restaurant                                   Cost

Activities                                   Cost


The best deal of the day                     Cost


The worst deal of the day                    Cost



Today's Adventures

Date _____     Mileage start _____

Weather today _____     Mileage end _____

Fueled at _____ Price _____     Odometer reading _____


We stayed at _____     Cost _____

This was a great place because _____

_____

_____

It could use some help in these areas _____

_____

_____

_____

We met _____     From where _____

Address and phone number _____

_____

_____

_____

Groceries                                        Cost

Restaurant                                       Cost

Activities                                       Cost


The best deal of the day                         Cost


The worst deal of the day                        Cost


Today's Adventures

## TRAVEL LOG

Date _____     Mileage start _____

Weather today _____     Mileage end _____

Fueled at _____ Price _____     Odometer reading _____


We stayed at _____     Cost _____

This was a great place because _____

_____

_____

It could use some help in these areas _____

_____

_____

We met _____     From where _____

Address and phone number _____

_____

_____

_____

Groceries                                      Cost

Restaurant                                      Cost

Activities                                      Cost


The best deal of the day                        Cost


The worst deal of the day                       Cost


Today's Adventures

## TRAVEL LOG

Date                                          Mileage start

Weather today                                 Mileage end

Fueled at                    Price            Odometer reading


We stayed at                                  Cost

This was a great place because




It could use some help in these areas




We met                                        From where

Address and phone number

Groceries                                           Cost

Restaurant                                          Cost

Activities                                          Cost


The best deal of the day                            Cost


The worst deal of the day                           Cost


Today's Adventures

## TRAVEL LOG

Date                                          Mileage start

Weather today                                 Mileage end

Fueled at                    Price            Odometer reading


We stayed at                                  Cost

This was a great place because




It could use some help in these areas




We met                                        From where

Address and phone number

Groceries                                    Cost

Restaurant                                   Cost

Activities                                   Cost


The best deal of the day                     Cost


The worst deal of the day                    Cost


Today's Adventures

## TRAVEL LOG

Date                                              Mileage start

Weather today                                     Mileage end

Fueled at              Price                      Odometer reading


We stayed at                                      Cost

This was a great place because



It could use some help in these areas




We met                                            From where

Address and phone number

Groceries                               Cost

Restaurant                              Cost

Activities                               Cost


The best deal of the day                Cost


The worst deal of the day               Cost


Today's Adventures

## TRAVEL LOG

Date _____          Mileage start _____

Weather today _____          Mileage end _____

Fueled at _____ Price _____          Odometer reading _____

We stayed at _____          Cost _____

This was a great place because _____

_____

_____

It could use some help in these areas _____

_____

_____

_____

We met _____          From where _____

Address and phone number _____

_____

_____

_____

Groceries                                          Cost

Restaurant                                         Cost

Activities                                         Cost


The best deal of the day                           Cost


The worst deal of the day                          Cost


Today's Adventures

## TRAVEL LOG

Date                                           Mileage start

Weather today                       Mileage end

Fueled at            Price             Odometer reading

We stayed at                        Cost

This was a great place because

It could use some help in these areas

We met                                 From where

Address and phone number

| Groceries | Cost |
|---|---|
| Restaurant | Cost |
| Activities | Cost |

| The best deal of the day | Cost |
|---|---|

| The worst deal of the day | Cost |
|---|---|

Today's Adventures

## TRAVEL LOG

Date _____         Mileage start _____

Weather today _____         Mileage end _____

Fueled at _____ Price _____    Odometer reading _____


We stayed at _____         Cost _____

This was a great place because _____

_____

_____

It could use some help in these areas _____

_____

_____


We met _____          From where _____

Address and phone number _____

_____

_____

_____

_____

Groceries                                    Cost

Restaurant                                   Cost

Activities                                   Cost


The best deal of the day                     Cost


The worst deal of the day                    Cost


Today's Adventures

Date _____     Mileage start _____

Weather today _____     Mileage end _____

Fueled at _____     Price _____     Odometer reading _____


We stayed at _____     Cost _____

This was a great place because _____

_____

_____

It could use some help in these areas _____

_____

_____

We met _____     From where _____

Address and phone number _____

_____

_____

_____

Groceries                                    Cost

Restaurant                                   Cost

Activities                                   Cost


The best deal of the day                     Cost


The worst deal of the day                    Cost


Today's Adventures

## TRAVEL LOG

Date                                        Mileage start

Weather today                               Mileage end

Fueled at                    Price          Odometer reading


We stayed at                                Cost

This was a great place because




It could use some help in these areas




We met                                      From where

Address and phone number

Groceries                                         Cost

Restaurant                                        Cost

Activities                                        Cost


The best deal of the day                          Cost


The worst deal of the day                         Cost


Today's Adventures

## TRAVEL LOG

Date                                          Mileage start

Weather today                                 Mileage end

Fueled at                    Price            Odometer reading


We stayed at                                  Cost

This was a great place because

_____

_____

It could use some help in these areas

_____

_____

We met                                        From where

Address and phone number

_____

_____

_____

Groceries                                          Cost

Restaurant                                         Cost

Activities                                         Cost


The best deal of the day                           Cost


The worst deal of the day                          Cost


Today's Adventures

## TRAVEL LOG

Date                                          Mileage start

Weather today                                 Mileage end

Fueled at              Price                  Odometer reading


We stayed at                                  Cost

This was a great place because




It could use some help in these areas




We met                                        From where

Address and phone number

Groceries                                    Cost

Restaurant                                   Cost

Activities                                   Cost


The best deal of the day                     Cost


The worst deal of the day                    Cost


Today's Adventures

## TRAVEL LOG

Date

Mileage start

Weather today

Mileage end

Fueled at                    Price

Odometer reading

We stayed at                          Cost

This was a great place because

It could use some help in these areas

We met                          From where

Address and phone number

Groceries                                             Cost

Restaurant                                            Cost

Activities                                            Cost


The best deal of the day                              Cost


The worst deal of the day                             Cost


Today's Adventures

## TRAVEL LOG

Date _____

Mileage start _____

Weather today _____

Mileage end _____

Fueled at _____ Price _____

Odometer reading _____

We stayed at _____

Cost _____

This was a great place because _____

_____

It could use some help in these areas _____

_____

We met _____

From where _____

Address and phone number _____

_____

Groceries                                    Cost

Restaurant                                   Cost

Activities                                   Cost


The best deal of the day                     Cost


The worst deal of the day                    Cost


Today's Adventures

## TRAVEL LOG

Date                                                    Mileage start

Weather today                                           Mileage end

Fueled at                    Price                      Odometer reading


We stayed at                                            Cost

This was a great place because




It could use some help in these areas




We met                                                  From where

Address and phone number

Groceries                                    Cost

Restaurant                                   Cost

Activities                                   Cost


The best deal of the day                     Cost


The worst deal of the day                    Cost


Today's Adventures

## TRAVEL LOG

Date                                              Mileage start

Weather today                                     Mileage end

Fueled at                  Price                  Odometer reading


We stayed at                                      Cost

This was a great place because




It could use some help in these areas




We met                                            From where

Address and phone number

Groceries                               Cost

Restaurant                              Cost

Activities                              Cost


The best deal of the day                Cost


The worst deal of the day               Cost


Today's Adventures

## TRAVEL LOG

Date ................................................ Mileage start ................................

Weather today ............................... Mileage end .................................

Fueled at .................. Price .......... Odometer reading .........................

We stayed at ................................... Cost ...........................................

This was a great place because ...................................................................

................................................................................................................

................................................................................................................

It could use some help in these areas ...........................................................

................................................................................................................

................................................................................................................

We met ........................................... From where .................................

Address and phone number .........................................................................

................................................................................................................

................................................................................................................

................................................................................................................

Groceries                                    Cost

Restaurant                                   Cost

Activities                                   Cost


The best deal of the day                     Cost


The worst deal of the day                    Cost


Today's Adventures

## TRAVEL LOG

Date                                    Mileage start

Weather today                           Mileage end

Fueled at                Price          Odometer reading


We stayed at                            Cost

This was a great place because



It could use some help in these areas




We met                                  From where

Address and phone number

Groceries                                    Cost

Restaurant                                   Cost

Activities                                   Cost


The best deal of the day                     Cost


The worst deal of the day                    Cost


Today's Adventures

## TRAVEL LOG

Date _____    Mileage start _____

Weather today _____    Mileage end _____

Fueled at _____ Price _____    Odometer reading _____


We stayed at _____    Cost _____

This was a great place because _____

_____

_____

It could use some help in these areas _____

_____

_____


We met _____    From where _____

Address and phone number _____

_____

_____

_____

Groceries                                    Cost

Restaurant                                   Cost

Activities                                   Cost


The best deal of the day                     Cost


The worst deal of the day                    Cost


Today's Adventures

Date _____     Mileage start _____

Weather today _____     Mileage end _____

Fueled at _____ Price _____     Odometer reading _____


We stayed at _____     Cost _____

This was a great place because _____
_____

_____

It could use some help in these areas _____
_____

_____


We met _____     From where _____

Address and phone number _____
_____

_____

_____

Groceries                                    Cost

Restaurant                                   Cost

Activities                                   Cost


The best deal of the day                     Cost


The worst deal of the day                    Cost


Today's Adventures

## TRAVEL LOG

Date _____      Mileage start _____

Weather today _____      Mileage end _____

Fueled at _____ Price _____      Odometer reading _____

We stayed at _____      Cost _____

This was a great place because _____

_____

_____

It could use some help in these areas _____

_____

_____

We met _____      From where _____

Address and phone number _____

_____

_____

_____

Groceries                                          Cost

Restaurant                                          Cost

Activities                                          Cost


The best deal of the day                            Cost


The worst deal of the day                           Cost


Today's Adventures

## TRAVEL LOG

Date _____          Mileage start _____

Weather today _____          Mileage end _____

Fueled at _____ Price _____          Odometer reading _____


We stayed at _____          Cost _____

This was a great place because _____

_____

_____

It could use some help in these areas _____

_____

_____

We met _____          From where _____

Address and phone number _____

_____

_____

_____

Groceries                                    Cost

Restaurant                                   Cost

Activities                                   Cost


The best deal of the day                     Cost


The worst deal of the day                    Cost


Today's Adventures

## TRAVEL LOG

Date _____   Mileage start _____

Weather today _____   Mileage end _____

Fueled at _____ Price _____   Odometer reading _____


We stayed at _____   Cost _____

This was a great place because _____

_____

_____

It could use some help in these areas _____

_____

_____

_____

We met _____   From where _____

Address and phone number _____

_____

_____

_____

_____

Groceries                                    Cost

Restaurant                                    Cost

Activities                                    Cost


The best deal of the day                      Cost


The worst deal of the day                     Cost


Today's Adventures

## TRAVEL LOG

Date _____     Mileage start _____

Weather today _____     Mileage end _____

Fueled at _____ Price _____    Odometer reading _____

We stayed at _____     Cost _____

This was a great place because _____

_____

It could use some help in these areas _____

_____

_____

We met _____     From where _____

Address and phone number _____

_____

_____

_____

Groceries                                    Cost

Restaurant                                   Cost

Activities                                   Cost


The best deal of the day                     Cost


The worst deal of the day                    Cost


Today's Adventures

## TRAVEL LOG

Date                                          Mileage start

Weather today                                 Mileage end

Fueled at                 Price               Odometer reading


We stayed at                                  Cost

This was a great place because



It could use some help in these areas



We met                                        From where

Address and phone number

Groceries                                    Cost

Restaurant                                   Cost

Activities                                   Cost


The best deal of the day                     Cost


The worst deal of the day                    Cost


Today's Adventures

## TRAVEL LOG

Date                                    Mileage start

Weather today                           Mileage end

Fueled at              Price            Odometer reading


We stayed at                            Cost

This was a great place because



It could use some help in these areas




We met                                  From where

Address and phone number

Groceries                               Cost

Restaurant                              Cost

Activities                              Cost


The best deal of the day                Cost


The worst deal of the day               Cost


Today's Adventures

## TRAVEL LOG

Date _____ Mileage start _____

Weather today _____ Mileage end _____

Fueled at _____ Price _____ Odometer reading _____

We stayed at _____ Cost _____

This was a great place because _____

_____

_____

It could use some help in these areas _____

_____

_____

We met _____ From where _____

Address and phone number _____

_____

_____

_____

Groceries                                    Cost

Restaurant                                   Cost

Activities                                   Cost


The best deal of the day                     Cost


The worst deal of the day                    Cost


Today's Adventures

## TRAVEL LOG

Date                                          Mileage start

Weather today                                 Mileage end

Fueled at                 Price              Odometer reading


We stayed at                                  Cost

This was a great place because



It could use some help in these areas



We met                                        From where

Address and phone number

Groceries                                     Cost

Restaurant                                    Cost

Activities                                    Cost


The best deal of the day              Cost


The worst deal of the day           Cost


Today's Adventures

# TRAVEL LOG

Date

Weather today

Fueled at                    Price

Mileage start

Mileage end

Odometer reading

We stayed at                                    Cost

This was a great place because

It could use some help in these areas

We met                                    From where

Address and phone number

Groceries                                    Cost

Restaurant                                   Cost

Activities                                   Cost


The best deal of the day                     Cost


The worst deal of the day                    Cost


Today's Adventures

## TRAVEL LOG

Date _____     Mileage start _____

Weather today _____     Mileage end _____

Fueled at _____ Price _____  Odometer reading _____


We stayed at _____     Cost _____

This was a great place because _____

_____

_____

It could use some help in these areas _____

_____

_____

_____

We met _____     From where _____

Address and phone number _____

_____

_____

_____

_____

Groceries                                    Cost

Restaurant                                    Cost

Activities                                    Cost


The best deal of the day                      Cost


The worst deal of the day                     Cost


Today's Adventures

## TRAVEL LOG

Date                                              Mileage start

Weather today                                     Mileage end

Fueled at                    Price                Odometer reading


We stayed at                                      Cost

This was a great place because




It could use some help in these areas




We met                                            From where

Address and phone number

Groceries                                    Cost

Restaurant                                   Cost

Activities                                   Cost


The best deal of the day              Cost


The worst deal of the day            Cost


Today's Adventures

## TRAVEL LOG

Date _____

Weather today _____

Fueled at _____ Price _____

We stayed at _____

This was a great place because _____

_____

_____

It could use some help in these areas _____

_____

_____

_____

We met _____

Address and phone number _____

_____

_____

_____

Mileage start _____

Mileage end _____

Odometer reading _____

Cost _____

From where _____

Groceries                                    Cost

Restaurant                                   Cost

Activities                                   Cost


The best deal of the day                     Cost


The worst deal of the day                    Cost


Today's Adventures

## TRAVEL LOG

Date _____     Mileage start _____

Weather today _____     Mileage end _____

Fueled at _____ Price _____     Odometer reading _____


We stayed at _____     Cost _____

This was a great place because _____

_____

_____

It could use some help in these areas _____

_____

_____

We met _____     From where _____

Address and phone number _____

_____

_____

_____

Groceries                              Cost

Restaurant                             Cost

Activities                             Cost


The best deal of the day               Cost


The worst deal of the day              Cost


Today's Adventures

## TRAVEL LOG

Date                                    Mileage start

Weather today                           Mileage end

Fueled at              Price            Odometer reading

We stayed at                            Cost

This was a great place because

It could use some help in these areas

We met                                  From where

Address and phone number

Groceries                                    Cost

Restaurant                                   Cost

Activities                                   Cost


The best deal of the day                     Cost


The worst deal of the day                    Cost


Today's Adventures

## TRAVEL LOG

Date _____          Mileage start _____

Weather today _____          Mileage end _____

Fueled at _____          Price _____          Odometer reading _____


We stayed at _____          Cost _____

This was a great place because _____

_____

_____

It could use some help in these areas _____

_____

_____

We met _____          From where _____

Address and phone number _____

_____

_____

_____

Groceries                                 Cost

Restaurant                                 Cost

Activities                                 Cost


The best deal of the day                   Cost


The worst deal of the day                  Cost


Today's Adventures

## TRAVEL LOG

Date _____

Weather today _____

Fueled at _____ Price _____

Mileage start _____

Mileage end _____

Odometer reading _____

We stayed at _____

This was a great place because _____

_____

_____

It could use some help in these areas _____

_____

_____

We met _____

Address and phone number _____

_____

_____

_____

Cost _____

From where _____

Groceries                                    Cost

Restaurant                                    Cost

Activities                                    Cost


The best deal of the day                      Cost


The worst deal of the day                     Cost



Today's Adventures

## TRAVEL LOG

Date _____                    Mileage start _____

Weather today _____          Mileage end _____

Fueled at _____ Price _____           Odometer reading _____

We stayed at _____             Cost _____

This was a great place because _____

_____

_____

It could use some help in these areas _____

_____

_____

We met _____                   From where _____

Address and phone number _____

_____

_____

_____

Groceries                                    Cost

Restaurant                                   Cost

Activities                                   Cost


The best deal of the day                     Cost


The worst deal of the day                    Cost


Today's Adventures

## TRAVEL LOG

Date _____ Mileage start _____

Weather today _____ Mileage end _____

Fueled at _____ Price ____ Odometer reading _____


We stayed at _____ Cost _____

This was a great place because _____

_____

_____

It could use some help in these areas _____

_____

_____

We met _____ From where _____

Address and phone number _____

_____

_____

_____

Groceries                                    Cost

Restaurant                                   Cost

Activities                                   Cost


The best deal of the day                     Cost


The worst deal of the day                    Cost


Today's Adventures

## TRAVEL LOG

Date _____    Mileage start _____

Weather today _____    Mileage end _____

Fueled at _____ Price ____    Odometer reading _____


We stayed at _____    Cost _____

This was a great place because _____

_____

_____

It could use some help in these areas _____

_____

_____

We met _____    From where _____

Address and phone number _____

_____

_____

_____

Groceries                                    Cost

Restaurant                                   Cost

Activities                                   Cost


The best deal of the day                     Cost


The worst deal of the day                    Cost


Today's Adventures